COPYMASTERS

FOR THE

OBSERVATION SURVEY

REVISED SECOND EDITION

MARIE M. CLAY

HEINEMANN
Portsmouth, NH

Heinemann
A division of Reed Elsevier, Inc.
361 Hanover Street
Portsmouth, NH 03801-3912
www.heinemann.com

Offices and agents throughout the world

Originally published by Heinemann Education, a division of Reed Publishing (NZ) Ltd, 39 Rawene Road, Birkenhead, Auckland, New Zealand. Associated companies, branches, and representatives throughout the world.

ISBN: 978-0-325-01141-7 (USA)
ISBN: 0-86944-647-X (NZ)

© 2007, 2002 Marie M. Clay

Printed in the United States of America on acid-free paper
11 10 09 08 07 VP 1 2 3 4 5

Contents

Sand	
Stones	☐
Moon	☐
Shoes	☐

CONCEPTS ABOUT PRINT SCORE SHEET

Date: _____

Name: _____ Age: _____ TEST SCORE: [   ] /24

Recorder: _____ Date of Birth: _____ STANINE GROUP: [   ]

PAGE	SCORE	ITEM	COMMENT
Cover		1. Front of book	
2/3		2. Print contains message	
4/5		3. Where to start	
4/5		4. Which way to go	
4/5		5. Return sweep to left	
4/5		6. Word-by-word matching	
6		7. First and last concept	
7		8. Bottom of picture	
8/9		9. Begins 'The' (Sand)	
		Begins 'I' (Stones)	
		Begins 'I' (Moon)	
		Begins 'Leaves' (Shoes)	
		bottom line, then top, OR turns book	
10/11		10. Line order altered	
12/13		11. Left page before right	
12/13		12. One change in word order	
12/13		13. One change in letter order	
14/15		14. One change in letter order	
14/15		15. Meaning of a question mark	
16/17		16. Meaning of full stop (period)	
16/17		17. Meaning of comma	
16/17		18. Meaning of quotation marks	
16/17		19. Locate: m h (Sand); t b (Stones);	
		m i (Moon); m i (Shoes)	
18/19		20. Reversible words 'was', 'no'	
20		21. One letter: two letters	
20		22. One word: two words	
20		23. First and last letter of word	
20		24. Capital letter	

RUNNING RECORD SHEET

Name: _____ Date: _____ D. of B.: _____ Age: _____ yrs _____ mths

School: _____ Recorder: _____

Text Titles	Errors Running Words	Error Ratio	Accuracy Rate	Self-correction Ratio
Easy _____	_____	1: _____	_____ %	1: _____
Instructional _____	_____	1: _____	_____ %	1: _____
Hard _____	_____	1: _____	_____ %	1: _____

Directional movement _____

Analysis of Errors and Self-corrections
Information used or neglected [Meaning (M), Structure or Syntax (S), Visual (V)]

Easy _____

Instructional _____

_____

Hard _____

_____

Cross-checking on information (Note that this behaviour changes over time)

		Count		Analysis of Errors and Self-corrections	
				Information used	
Page	Title	E	SC	E MSV	SC MSV

Page		Count		Analysis of Errors and Self-corrections
				Information used
		E	SC	E MSV / SC MSV

RECORD OF BOOK LEVEL

Name: _____

Date of Birth: _____

Book Level	Enter examples of titles here																										
∴																										
⋮																										
24																										
23																										
22																										
21																										
20																										
19																										
18																										
17																										
16																										
15																										
14																										
13																										
12																										
11																										
10																										
9																										
8																										
7																										
6																										
5																										
4																										
3																										
2																										
1																										
0																										
Date																										

Gradient of Text Difficulty (Teacher Devised)

Weekly Observations

○ 90% accuracy or above
● below 90% accuracy

Record of Book Level Sheet   © Marie M. Clay   *Copymasters for the Observation Survey, Revised Second Edition* 2007

LETTER IDENTIFICATION SCORE SHEET
(ENGLISH)

Date: _____

Name: _____   Age: _____   TEST SCORE: | /54 |

Recorder: _____   Date of Birth: _____   STANINE GROUP: | |

	A	S	Word	I.R.		A	S	Word	I.R.
A					a				
F					f				
K					k				
P					p				
W					w				
Z					z				
B					b				
H					h				
O					o				
J					j				
U					u				
					a				
C					c				
Y					y				
L					l				
Q					q				
M					m				
D					d				
N					n				
S					s				
X					x				
I					i				
E					e				
G					g				
R					r				
V					v				
T					t				
					g				
			TOTALS						

Confusions:

Letters Unknown:

Comment:

Recording:
A   Alphabet response: tick (check)
S   Letter-sound response: tick (check)
Word   Record the word the child gives
I.R.   Incorrect response: Record what the child says

TOTAL SCORE | |

WORD READING SCORE SHEET

Use any **one** list of words

Date: _____

Name: _____

TEST SCORE: [ ] /15

Age: _____ Date of Birth: _____

STANINE GROUP: [ ]

Recorder: _____

Record incorrect responses beside word

LIST **A**	LIST **B**	LIST **C**
I	and	Father
Mother	to	come
are	will	for
here	look	a
me	he	you
shouted	up	at
am	like	school
with	in	went
car	where	get
children	Mr	we
help	going	they
not	big	ready
too	go	this
meet	let	boys
away	on	please

Word Reading Score Sheet © Marie M. Clay *Copymasters for the Observation Survey, Revised Second Edition* 2007

WRITING VOCABULARY OBSERVATION SHEET

Date: _____

Name: _____   Age: _____

Recorder: _____   Date of Birth: _____

(Fold heading under before child uses sheet)

TEST SCORE: [   ]

STANINE GROUP: [   ]

WRITING VOCABULARY WEEKLY RECORD SHEET

Name: _____

Date of Birth: _____

Initial Testing: Date:	Week: Date:	Week: Date:	Week: Date:	Week: Date:
	Week: Date:	Week: Date:	Week: Date:	Week: Date:

HEARING AND RECORDING SOUNDS IN WORDS
OBSERVATION SHEET

Date: _____

Name: _____   Age: _____

Recorder: _____   Date of Birth: _____

TEST SCORE: [ ] /37

STANINE GROUP: [ ]

(Fold heading under before child uses sheet)

OBSERVATION SURVEY SUMMARY SHEET

Name: _____ Date: _____ D. of B.: _____ Age: _____ yrs _____ mths

School: _____ Recorder: _____

Text Titles		Errors / Running Words	Error Ratio	Accuracy Rate	Self-correction Ratio
Easy	_____	_____	1: _____	_____ %	1: _____
Instructional	_____	_____	1: _____	_____ %	1: _____
Hard	_____	_____	1: _____	_____ %	1: _____

Directional movement _____

Analysis of Errors and Self-corrections
Information used or neglected [Meaning (M), Structure or Syntax (S), Visual (V)]

Easy _____

Instructional _____

_____

Hard _____

_____

Cross-checking on information (Note that this behaviour changes over time)

_____

How the reading sounds	Easy			
	Instructional			
	Hard			
			Raw Score	Stanine
Letter Identi-fication				
Concepts About Print	* Sand Stones Shoes Moon			
Word Reading	* List A List B List C Other _____ (Enter test name)			
Writing Vocabulary				
Hearing and Recording Sounds in Words	* A B C D E			
Other tasks	Writing sample Story Spelling			

* Circle whatever was used

 Copymasters for the Observation Survey, Revised Second Edition 2007

An Analysis of the Child's Strategic Activity

Useful strategic activity on text:

Problem strategic activity on text:

Useful strategic activity with words:

Problem strategic activity with words:

Useful strategic activity with letters:

Problem strategic activity with letters:

Summary statement:

Signature: _____

OBSERVATION SUMMARY FOR MULTIPLE ASSESSMENTS

Name: _____

Date of Birth: _____

School: _____

SUMMARY OF RUNNING RECORD

Text Titles	Errors / Running words	Error Ratio	Accuracy Rate	Self-correction Ratio

Initial Assessment   Date: _____

1. Easy _____ _____ 1: _____ _____ %: 1: _____

2. Instructional _____ _____ 1: _____ _____ %: 1: _____

3. Hard _____ _____ 1: _____ _____ %: 1: _____

Reassessment   Date: _____

1. Easy _____ _____ 1: _____ _____ %: 1: _____

2. Instructional _____ _____ 1: _____ _____ %: 1: _____

3. Hard _____ _____ 1: _____ _____ %: 1: _____

Further Assessment   Date: _____

1. Easy _____ _____ 1: _____ _____ %: 1: _____

2. Instructional _____ _____ 1: _____ _____ %: 1: _____

3. Hard _____ _____ 1: _____ _____ %: 1: _____

ASSESSMENT	L.I. 54	Stanine	C.A.P. 24	Stanine	Word Reading 15	Stanine	Other Reading Test Score	Writing Vocabulary No.	Stanine	Hearing Sounds in Words 37	Stanine
Initial assessment Date:											
Reassessment Date:											
Further Assessment (1)											
Further Assessment (2)											

RECOMMENDATIONS: (for class teacher, or for review, or further teaching, or further assessment)